The Gospel Primer No. 2

Published by
Pilgrims Books
Altamont, TN 37305

A is for **Ark**, t'was a wonderful boat,
Built in the wild, seething waters
to float.
Sin ruled in the hearts of the children
of men;
Vainly God warned them, again and
again.

Violence covered the land with its blood
Till all the earth was o'erwhelmed with a flood.
Black grew the sky in the tempest's dark path,
Trembled old earth in the hurricane's wrath;

Red glared the lightnings, and fierce fell the rain,
But o'er the wild, heaving, billowy main,
God kept them safe in that wonderful bark,—
Noah and his family,—safe in the Ark.

Genesis 7:23.

B stands for **Balaam,** of him I will
tell,—
Of Balaam the prophet,—and Balak as
well.
"Up," said the king to the prophet,
"behold,
I will enrich thee with silver and gold,

If thou wilt curse me these people who stand
Now on the shores of the Moabites' land."
Then came the Lord to the prophet, and said,
"Thou shalt not curse them,—but bless them instead."

"Nay," said the prophet, "behold ye shall bring
Saddle and bridle; I'll haste to the King."
But wonder of wonders! the Lord puts a word
In the mouth of the beast; and the prophet has heard

Numbers 22:28.

C stands for **Canaan;** 'tis here we are told,
Israel was led in the good days of old.
Out from the bondage of Egypt's dark land,
Led by the strength of the Almighty's hand;

Out of the darkness, and out of the night,
Out of their toil with the strength of His might.
Far from the armies of Pharaoh, led
By the Pillar of Fire that shone overhead.

Oh, the great miracles wrought by the Lord,—
Wrought by the strength of His wonderful word!
Safely He led them through many a snare,
Into the borders of Canaan so fair.

Deuteronomy 34:4.

D is for **David;** now list while I sing
Of the psalmist of Israel, prophet and king:
His father was Jesse; and David did keep—
Since he was the youngest—his dear father's sheep.

One night from the wilderness—thus we are told—
A gaunt lion came, that was hungry and bold;
And again a fierce bear that was growling and grim,
Came prowling along 'mong the shadows so dim.

Then David arose, though a stripling so fair,
And slew he the lion, and slew he the bear.
He killed a brave giant with naught but a sling,
And Samuel the prophet anointed him king.

1 Samuel 17:34-51.

E is for **Eden,** the garden of God;
Where our first parents in innocence trod
O'er the sweet dale on the fresh, verdant sod.
Sparkling fountains and rivers so bright,
Murmured sweet songs in this home of delight.
Sweetly content were the first happy pair,
Breathing the perfume of life-giving air,—
Adam so brave, and the woman so fair.

But to this garden the serpent crept in,
Bringing the legions of sorrow and sin,
Breathing decay with his poisonous breath,
Bringing in misery, anguish, and death.

Genesis 2:8; 3:1–24.

F is for **Famine** that Joseph foretold
By the dream of king Pharaoh in Egypt of old.
The seven fat kine and the seven good ears
As seen in the vision, were bountiful years;
While the seven bad ears, and the kine that were lean,
Which in the strange dream of the monarch were seen,
Were seven years' famine, where nothing would grow
In the dry, barren ground, though the husbandmen sow.

Then Joseph made haste, by the word of the king,
And into the garners of Egypt did bring
Good corn in abundance, and kept it in store
That the people might eat while the famine was sore.

Genesis 41:14–57.

G is **Gethsemane's** Garden where trod
Jesus, the Son of the Infinite God.
Ah! His deep anguish we never may know,
Bearing earth's burden of sin and of woe.

There mid the solitude dim and profound,
Sweat-drops of agony moistened the ground.
Up from the valley of Kedron below,
Cometh the bands of the treacherous foe,—

Cometh false Judas with staves and with sword,—
Comes to betray Him,—his suffering Lord.
Soon to Golgotha, behold Him again,
Giving His life for the children of men!

Mark 14:32–45; 15–38.

H stands for the name of a monarch of old,
Good king **Hezekiah,** and thus we are told;
His father, King Ahaz, was wicked and vile,   [defile.
And caused all the people the land to

But the idols so vile, Hezekiah laid low,
And none but the true God of heaven would know.
At last he was sick, and 'twas said he must die,
But he turned to the wall, and with pitiful cry,

He begged of the Lord to restore him again
That he might sing praise 'mong the children of men.
So the Lord heard his prayer, and He pitied his tears,
And prolonged the king's life fifteen wonderful years.

2 Kings 20:1–12.

I is for **Ishmael**, Abraham's son,—
  Brother of Isaac, the dutiful one.
But unto Hager, his mother, the Lord
Sent by His angel this wonderous
  word:—

"Thy son," saith Jehovah, "a wild
  man shall be,"
So he dwelt in the forest,—an archer was he.
One day, when they wandered,—the mother and child,—
Afar from their home, in the desert so wild,

Their water was spent, and with sorrowful cry,
She laid her son down, in the desert to die.
But God heard the cry of the perishing child,
And saved him from death in the desert so wild.

Genesis 21:14-22.

J is for **Jonah**; the Lord bade him go
  With a message of warning to
  Israels foe.
But the prophet rebelled, and for Tar-
  shish set sail,
When, down on the sea came a terrible
  gale.

But when from the vessel the prophet was cast,
The waves ceased to rage, and were quiet at last.
Then the seamen beheld, while their faces grew white
And their knees shook with terror, a wonderful sight.

Behold a great whale on the crest of the wave,
And it swallowed the prophet, and no man could save.
But God touched the fish, and He gave it command,—
And it vomited Jonah up on the dry land.

Jonah 1:1-17.

K stands for **Kohath** and for Korah
as well;
Now listen to me while a story I tell:
This Korah rebelled in the days long
ago
When Israel journeyed to Canaan, you
know.

And with Dathan, Abiram, and others, they said,
"Pray, why should this people by Moses be led?"
Said Korah, "We also are righteous, as he,
Why sitteth he higher in judgment than we?"

But Moses, indeed, was a prophet of God,
And He visits these men with a chastening rod.
With loud wails of anguish,—a terrible sound,—
The earth ope's her mouth, and they sink in the ground.

Numbers 16:1–36.

L stands for **Leprosy**; emblem of
sin;
Vile and corrupt, both without and
within.
But with one look, and with one swift
command,   [ter's hand,
One cleansing touch from the dear Mas-

Matters it not how corrupted with sin,
Matters it not how defiled we have been,
Jesus can heal and the captive set free,—
Wonderful, wonderful Healer is He.

Once on the verge of a leperous grave,
Ten wretched lepers besought Him to save;
Loathsome and outcast, unclean and defiled,
Their flesh was made fair as the flesh of a child.

Luke 17:12–19.

M is for **Manna**; come list while I tell
Of the wonderful bread from the heavens, which fell:—
For forty long years every morning 'twas found,   [ered the ground,—
For 'twas sent every night, and it cov-

Save only the Sabbath; for that day was blest,—
Both in earing and harvest the people must rest.
Now the Manna was white, and 'twas small, round, and sweet,
'Twas the food which the angels in heaven did eat.

What a wonderful thing that this Manna should fall
In the camp of God's people to nourish them all!
And yet did they grieve Him,—these hard-hearted men,
And still He forgave them, again and again.

Exodus 16:4-9.

N stands for the name of a monarch of old,
The great king of Babylon, mighty and bold;
King **Nebuchadnezzar,** and thus we are told:—   [strength of his pride,
One day while he walked in the

And thought of his mighty dominions so wide,
He said in his heart, as he gazed o'er the land,
Is not this great Babylon, built by mine hand—
By the strength of my might, and my glory so grand?

Then quick came a voice from the far distant heaven:
"O Nebuchadnezzar, to thee it is given;
Like a beast of the field thou shalt graze on the sod,
Until thou shalt know that Jehovah is God!"

Daniel 4:30-34.   [9]

O stands for **Og,** who was Israel's foe,—
The great king of Bashan in days long ago,—
The prince over sixty vast cities was he,— [mighty to see.
A prince fierce and dreadful, and
And he was a wonderful warrior as well;
But quick before Israel's armies he fell.
Now Og was a giant; pray, have you not read
That eight cubits long was the length of his bed?

And 'twas four cubits wide, and of iron was made,—
'Twas the bed of a giant who was not afraid.
But ah, he was slain, for 'tis thus we are told,—
Both he and king Sihon the Amorite bold.

Deuteronomy 3:11.

P is for **Peter;** come list while I tell
Of this bold disciple and that which befell
Poor Peter Bar-jona, long time ago, when
The wonderful Saviour was here among men:

One night, with his comrades, on deep Galilee,
When the fierce winds came down on the face of the sea,
In fright they beheld amid tempest and storm,
Far out on the waves a misterious form.

And when Peter saw 'twas the Master, he cried,
"O bid me come, blessed Lord, to thy side."
But beginning to sink in the treacherous wave,
He cried to the Lord to have mercy and save.

Matthew 14:24-32.

Q is for **Quails** that were sent long
ago
For Israel's food in the desert you
know.
For the people had murmured with
bitter complaint: [hungry and faint;
"We loathe this light food, and are
We long for the flesh-pots," the multitude shrieks,—
The flesh-pots of Egypt, the garlics and leeks.
Appoint, O appoint us a leader, we pray,
We'll go back to Egypt and make no delay.

Were there no graves in Egypt, that we should be brought
To this dreary desert to perish for naught?"
So the Lord sent them quails, in their anger and pride,
And the people did eat until scores of them died.

Numbers 11:31–34.

R stands for the name of the sweet
gleaner, **Ruth,**
A fair Moabitess of beauty and truth.
I will tell you of her, if you'll listen
to me,—
The daughter-in-law of Naomi was she.

Now she loved her good mother, and earnestly plead;
"Entreat me not ever to leave thee," she said.
"Thy people, *my* people shall evermore be,
And thy God, be *my* God, forever," said she.

And so, with her grain sack she wended her way
To the fields of good Boaz, and gleaned every day.
And she lived a devoted and dutiful life,
And Boaz of Bethlehem made her his wife.

Ruth 1:16; 2:1–23; 4:10.

S is for **Sabbath,** sweet Sabbath of rest,
Which God at creation both honored and blest;
For when all the work of His hand was complete, [peaceful and sweet.
The calm, blessed Sabbath dawned

Ah, bright were the flowers, and green was the sod,
When Eden bloomed fresh from the hand of its God.
The six working days of creation were passed,
And the seventh—the Sabbath of rest—came at last.

Ah, sacred, and sanctified, changeless, and blest,
Is the sweet, peaceful Sabbath—the Sabbath of rest;
And e'en while the years of eternity flow,
The same blessed Sabbath of rest shall we know.

Genesis 2:1-3. Isaiah 66:22, 23.

T stands for the **Treasures** the Magi did bring,
When the star led them on, to the sweet Infant King;
And when they had found Him—the babe that they sought—
They gave Him the gold and the treasures they brought.

There was sweet frankincense from their far, distant land,
And much costly myrrh did they bring in their hand,
And spread it before Him, with silver and gold,
And they worshiped the Saviour,—these princes of old.

O wonderful Babe, and O wonderful star
That shone on the wise men and led them afar;
And glorious tidings that herald the birth
Of Jesus, Redeemer, and Saviour of earth.

Matthew 2:9-12.

U standeth for **Uz,** where in days long ago,
The servant of God had his dwelling, you know.
A just man was he, both to great and to small; [a wall.
And around him Jehovah had builded

Then the Lord said to Satan: "Pray do you not see
My good servant Job, how devoted is he?"
But the devil made answer: "Put forth now Thine hand
And touch all he hath,—all he hath in the land,

And behold he will curse thee e'en unto Thy face,
And bring Thy brave servant to deepest disgrace."
So the Lord tried the strength of the enemy's word;
But poor Job bore the test, and was true to the Lord.
Job 1:1-22, and onward.

V stands for the name of a beautiful queen,
As modest and dainty as ever was seen;
Her name was Queen **Vashti,** perhaps you have heard
How the king gave command, but she feared not his word.

Then the king in his anger and jealousy said,
"Go, take ye the crown—take the crown from her head.
My beautiful queen she shall nevermore be;
I'll choose me another, still fairer than she."

So Esther was chosen, good Mordecai's ward,
And Esther was trained in the fear of the Lord.
To the throne of the monarch the maiden was brought,
And through her, a mighty deliverance God wrought.
Esther 1:10-20; 8:15-17. [13]

W is for **Wilderness**, darksome and dim,
From whence came two bears that were horrid and grim.
And there was a prophet, Elijah by name,   [flame.
Who rode to the skies in a chariot of

Now his servant Elisha beheld him arise
With the horsemen of God to the far-away skies.
And this man Elisha was walking one day,
When a group of bad children were passing that way

"Go up, O thou bald-head! Go up now," they cry,
"Go up, like thy master, go up to the sky!"
Then these two hungry bruin arose from their lairs;
And forty-two children were torn by the bears!

2 Kings 2:11–25.

X is the numeral standing for "ten,"—
The Ten great Commandments that God gave to men.
On Sinai's mount the great Lawgiver came,   [fire and flame.
And the top of the mount burned with

Now Moses remained in that glorious place,
Till the splendor shone bright from the skin of his face.
The Almighty came down from His heavenly throne,
And wrote with His finger on tables of stone

That wonderful law which can ne'er pass away
Though the earth and its treasures wax old and decay.
It cannot be changed,—it is perfect and broad,
And firm as the throne of the Infinite God.

Exodus 20:1–18; Matthew 5:18; Luke 16:17;
Psalms 119:6.

Y is for **Youth** who was killed by
a fall,
As he sat in the window high up in
the wall,
To list to the wonderful preaching of
Paul. [stirred,
For the soul of the mighty apostle was

And he went everywhere that he might preach the word.
And his heart was so filled with his message so great,
That he recked not at all that the hour was late;
So he preached all one night, till the dim shadows gray
Betokened the near coming dawn of the day.

And a young man named Eutychus, dropping asleep,
Fell out of the window in slumber so deep,—
Fell down, and was killed by the terrible fall;
But God brought him to life through the praying of Paul.

Acts 20:8–12.

Z is for **Zacchaeus,** a small man
was he,
Who, to see the dear Lord, climbed a
sycamore tree.
He had longed to see Jesus, by night
and by day, [by that way,
And so when he heard that He passed

He said, "If I climb up this sycamore tall,
I shall see His dear face, even though I *am* small."
So he climbed up the tree, 'mong the branches so green,
Till the well-beloved form of the Master was seen.

And then,—O what joy filled his bosom, for see,—
The dear Lord is calling him down from the tree.
So let us, like Zacchaeus, list to His word,
And haste to receive Him,—our Master and Lord.

Luke 19:1–7.

The Creation.

"In the beginning God created the heaven and the earth." Genesis 1:1.

JESUS CHRIST is the Son of God, and bears the name of God. God and Christ are one in all their plans and in all their work.

Christ our Saviour is "the Word" of God. He speaks the word which creates all things. The Bible says that "all things were made by Him; and without Him was not any thing made that was made." See John 1:1-3.

When men make things they must have tools and material out of which to make them. It was not so with God when He made the earth. David said, "He spake and it was done." Psalm 33:9. When God speaks His word can do anything.

God created the earth and everything that lives and grows on it, in six days. He rested the seventh day, and looked over the work He had finished. Then He blessed it and made it His holy Sabbath.

When the Sabbath comes, He wants us to stop our work and play, and look at the beautiful things that are around us and remember that He made them for us. See Genesis 2:1-3; Exodus 20:8-11.

2

Driven from Eden.

"The Lord God sent him forth from the garden of Eden." Genesis 3 : 23.

AFTER God had created the world He made a beautiful home for Adam and Eve. He called it the garden of Eden.

In this garden grew all kinds of trees, herbs, grasses, and flowers. Upon the trees grew the most beautiful fruit.

The Lord told Adam and Eve that they could eat of the fruit of all the trees but one. If they should eat of "the tree of the knowledge of good and evil" they should "surely die."

But one day curiosity led Eve to go to the tree to see what it was like. When she came to it she found Satan there in the form of a serpent.

The serpent lied to Eve and told her that the fruit of the tree was good, and that she would not die if she ate of it. So Eve believed the serpent and ate of the fruit and gave some to Adam and he ate of it.

Then the Lord met them and told them that they had disobeyed Him and must leave their beautiful home, and that they would soon die. This was the way sin and death came into the world.

The Flood.

"I do bring a flood of waters upon the earth." Genesis 6 : 17.

BEFORE the flood men lived to be nearly a thousand years old. Living so long they became very wise and very wicked.

Because they were so wicked the Lord said He would send a flood and destroy man and everything that was on the earth.

But Noah was a good man, and the Lord told him to build a very large boat. In this boat, called the ark, God promised to save Noah and his family and some of all kinds of beasts.

It took Noah a hundred and twenty years to build the ark. When it was finished the Lord caused some of all kinds of animals to go into it. Then Noah and his family of eight people went in, and the Lord shut to the door.

When all were safe in the ark the Lord sent a terrible storm, and the waters flooded the earth till all the wicked men and all the beasts not in the ark were drowned.

For nearly half a year the waters covered the earth. Then the ark rested upon Mount Ararat. Then the Lord opened the door, and all that were in the ark came out. How glad they must have been to come again onto solid ground.

The Tower of Babel.

"And they said, Go to, let us build us a city and a tower, whose top may reach unto heaven." Genesis 11:4.

AFTER the flood there were only eight persons left in all the world. But in a little more than a hundred years this family of eight had become a great multitude.

Little by little they forgot the good teaching of Noah. They became very proud and wicked. They remembered the story of the flood, and feared there might be another.

So to protect themselves from another flood they began to build a great tower. This tower was to be so high that it would "reach unto heaven." Then if a flood should come they could run to it and be safe.

The Lord allowed them to go on until the tower was very large and high. Then He stopped the work of these wicked men.

Before that all men spoke the same language. But at this time the Lord changed their speech so that they spoke many languages.

Then the workmen could not understand what was said to them. So the confusion was so great that the work was stopped and the people were scattered. And this is how there came to be so many languages in the world. After this it was called the tower of Babel. Babel means confusion.

Abraham, Isaac, and Jacob.

"Now the Lord had said unto Abram, Get thee out of thy country,
and from thy kindred, and from thy father's house, unto a
land that I will show thee." Genesis 12 : I.

IN a little more than three hundred years after the
flood nearly all the world had forgotten God, and
had turned to the worship of idols.

But there was one man who was true to God. His
name was Abraham. But his father and his friends
worshiped idols made by men.

So the Lord told Abraham to leave his father's
house and go to the land of Canaan. The Lord promised to give him this land for a home, and that he
should be the father of a great nation.

Then Abraham took Lot, his nephew, and all their
flocks and herds, and journeyed to the land of promise.

When Abraham was about a hundred years old
he had a son named Isaac, whom he dearly loved. He
was a good man like his father, and served the true God.

Isaac had two sons, Jacob and Esau. When they
grew up there was trouble between them, and Jacob
had to go far from home and remain away for many years.

When he did return he had twelve sons. These
sons did not always agree, and were often unkind to
their father.

But the two younger sons, Joseph and Benjamin,
loved their father and were kind to their brothers.

Joseph's Dreams.

"And Joseph dreamed a dream, and he told it his brethren: and they hated him yet the more." Genesis 37:5.

JACOB loved Joseph more than any of his other children, "because he was the son of his old age." And he loved him the more because he was kind and obedient.

And he made Joseph a coat of many colors. But his brothers hated him and were jealous because of Jacob's great love for him.

When Joseph was seventeen years old he had a dream and told it to his brethren. He dreamed that they were all binding sheaves of grain in the field, and his sheaf stood upright, and their sheaves bowed down to his sheaf.

He did not know what the dream meant, but his brothers did. And they said, "Shalt thou indeed reign over us?" And they hated him the more because of the dream.

And again he dreamed that the sun and the moon and the eleven stars bowed down to him. And he told this dream to his father and to his brothers.

His father rebuked him, and said, "Shall I and thy mother and thy brethren indeed come to bow down ourselves to thee?" But these dreams came true a few years later.

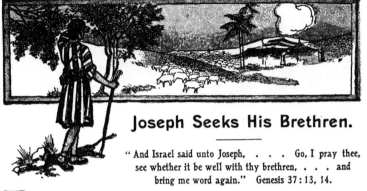

Joseph Seeks His Brethren.

" And Israel said unto Joseph, . . . Go, I pray thee, see whether it be well with thy brethren, . . . and bring me word again." Genesis 37 : 13, 14.

JOSEPH'S brothers were shepherds and cared for their father's flocks. Jacob had not heard from them for many days. So he sent Joseph to find them.

Joseph searched for them a long time, for they had removed to Dothan where the pasture was good. When his brothers saw him, they said:—

"Behold, this dreamer cometh. Come now therefore, and let us slay him, and cast him into some pit, and we will say, Some evil beast hath devoured him : and we shall see what will become of his dreams."

But Reuben did not like this wicked plan, and said, "Let us not kill him, . . . but cast him into this pit."

Then when his brothers had gone he intended to return and draw him out of the pit and send him back to his father.

All the brothers agreed to this plan. And they took from Joseph his coat of many colors, and cast him into the pit. Then they sat down to eat.

Sold as a Slave.

"Judah said, . . . Come, and let us sell him to the Ishmaelites." Genesis 37 : 26, 27.

SOON a caravan of Ishmaelites came that way. Then the brothers drew Joseph out of the pit and sold him to them for twenty pieces of silver.

And they took him with them to Egypt and sold him to a rich man as a slave.

After Joseph was gone the brothers began to feel guilty. How should they tell their father what they had done to Joseph?

So, to cover up their sin, they planned to tell their father a cruel falsehood. They killed a kid, and dipped Joseph's coat in the blood, and brought it to their father, and said:—

"This have we found: know now whether it be thy son's coat or no."

And he knew it, and said, "It is my son's coat; an evil beast hath devoured him."

"And Jacob rent his clothes, and put sackcloth upon his loins, and mourned for his son many days."

His children tried to comfort him, but could not. And Jacob said, "I will go down into the grave unto my son mourning."

Joseph in Prison.

"And Joseph's master took him, and put him into the prison." Genesis 39 : 20.

WHEN the Ishmaelites came to Egypt they sold Joseph to Potiphar, captain of the king's guard. And the Lord was with Joseph, so Potiphar made him overseer of all he had in the house and in the field.

A wicked lie was told about Joseph, so Potiphar put him in prison. But the Lord gave him favor with the jailor. And the care of everything in the prison was given to Joseph.

Now the king was displeased with his chief butler and baker, and cast them into the prison. One morning Joseph saw that they looked sad, and he asked them why they were so sorrowful.

They answered, "We have dreamed a dream, and there is no interpreter of it. And Joseph said unto them, Do not interpretations belong to God? tell me them, I pray you." And they told him.

God gave the right answer to Joseph, and he told them that the dreams meant that the king would soon take them from prison. One he would hang, and the other would go free. And it happened just as Joseph had said.

Joseph Before Pharaoh.

"Then Pharaoh sent and called Joseph, and they brought him hastily out of the dungeon." Genesis 41 : 14.

TWO years after the butler and baker had been taken from prison, the Lord gave Pharaoh two dreams.

In the first dream seven good, fat cattle came up out of the river. Then he saw seven poor, lean cattle come up. And the lean cattle ate up the fat ones.

In the second dream he saw seven good ears of grain on one stalk. Then he saw seven thin, blasted ears. And the blasted ears ate up the good ears.

These dreams troubled the king. So he sent for the wise men of Egypt to tell him the meaning of them, but they could not.

Then the chief butler remembered Joseph, and told the king how he had interpreted his dream, and that of the chief baker, when they were in prison together.

So the king sent for Joseph at once and told him the dreams. And Joseph said that the seven good cattle, and the seven good ears of grain, meant seven years of great plenty in Egypt.

And the seven thin cattle, and the seven blasted ears of grain, meant seven years of famine that were to follow the years of plenty.

Joseph Made Ruler of Egypt.

" And Pharaoh said unto Joseph, See, I have set thee over all the land
of Egypt." Genesis 41 : 41.

JOSEPH advised Pharaoh to select a man to gather grain during the seven good years, and store it up for food during the seven years of famine.

And Pharaoh chose Joseph to do this work because God was with him. And he put his royal seal-ring upon the hand of Joseph, and clothed him with kingly robes, and put a chain of gold about his neck.

"And he made him to ride in the second chariot which he had; and they cried before him, Bow the knee: and he made him ruler over all the land of Egypt."

At the end of the seven years of plenty the famine came on all the earth. But there was plenty in Egypt. And they came from all countries to buy.

It was not long until food became scarce in the house of Jacob, in the land of Canaan. So he sent his ten older sons to Egypt to buy grain.

Joseph knew his brothers, but they did not think that the powerful governor of Egypt was their brother whom they had sold about thirteen years before.

Joseph wanted to know if his brothers had become good men. So he put Simeon in prison, and let the others go back with food. But he told them they must bring Benjamin with them when they came again.

The Cup in Benjamin's Sack.

"And the cup was found in Benjamin's sack." Genesis 44 : 12.

WHEN the grain was nearly gone Jacob sent his sons to Egypt to buy more. Benjamin went with them this time.

When the brothers reached Egypt, Joseph brought Simeon to them from the prison, and made a great feast for them in his own house.

Then he told his steward to fill their sacks with grain, and to put every man's money in his sack. His drinking cup was also to be put in Benjamin's sack.

When they started for home, and had gone only a little way, Joseph sent an officer after them, who accused them of stealing the governor's cup.

But they denied it, and said that if it was found with any of them he should die, and the rest of them would be slaves. But the officer said, No, but the one with whom it is found shall be a slave to the governor, and the rest shall go home in peace.

So they searched, and were astonished to find the cup in Benjamin's sack. And they all went back in sorrow to see Joseph, the ruler of Egypt.

Judah's Plea for Benjamin.

"Let thy servant abide instead of the lad a bondman to my lord." Genesis 44 : 33.

WHEN the brethren came before Joseph, Judah made a most earnest plea for Benjamin. He asked that he might remain as a slave in Egypt, and Benjamin go back to his father.

All the brothers acted a noble part in their trouble. Joseph saw that they were changed men, and he was satisfied. So he sent away his Egyptian servants, and said to his brothers :—

"I am Joseph; doth my father yet live?" And he wept aloud.

"And his brethren could not answer him," for they were much afraid.

But Joseph did not want to harm his brothers, although they had been very wicked. He did not even want them to feel bad, so he said to them :—

"Now therefore be not grieved, nor angry with yourselves, that ye sold me hither: for God did send me before you to preserve life."

"So now it was not you that sent me hither, but God: and He hath made me a father to Pharaoh, and lord of all his house, and a ruler throughout all the land of Egypt."

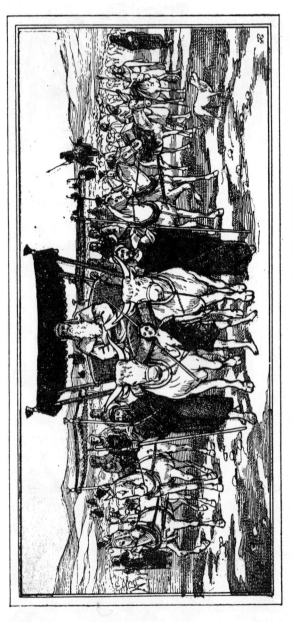

JACOB ON HIS JOURNEY TO EGYPT.

"And Israel took his journey with all that he had. . . And God spake unto Israel in the visions of the night, and said, . . . I will go down with thee into Egypt; and I will also surely bring thee up again: and Joseph shall put his hand upon thine eyes. . . And the sons of Israel carried Jacob their father, and their little ones, and their wives, in the wagons which Pharaoh had sent to carry him. And they took their cattle, and their goods, . . . and came into Egypt." Genesis 46: 1-6.

[30]

Jacob Comes to Egypt.

"And Israel took his journey with all that he had." Genesis 46 : 1.

AFTER Joseph had made himself known to his brethren, he said to them:—

"Haste ye, and go up to my father, and say unto him, Thus saith thy son Joseph, God hath made me lord of all Egypt: come down unto me, tarry not:

"And thou shalt dwell in the land of Goshen, . . . and there will I nourish thee; for yet there are five years of famine."

And Pharaoh gave them wagons and beasts to draw them, and sent presents to Jacob. And he sent him word to hasten and come to Egypt as Joseph had said.

When the brothers reached home and told Jacob, their father, he could not believe that Joseph still lived. But when he saw the wagons sent for him he knew it must be true.

"And Israel said, It is enough; Joseph my son is yet alive: I will go and see him before I die."

When they reached Goshen, Joseph met them with his chariot, and he fell on his father's neck and wept.

"And Israel said unto Joseph, Now let me die, since I have seen thy face, because thou art yet alive."

And so the dreams of Joseph came true.

Israel in Captivity.

"And the Egyptians made the children of Israel to serve with rigour: and they made their lives bitter with hard bondage, in mortar, and in brick, and in all manner of service in the field." Exodus 1 : 13, 14.

SOME time after the death of Joseph there arose a new king in Egypt who knew not Joseph. He did not choose to acknowledge all the good which Joseph had done to the whole land.

But he did see that the family of Jacob had increased to a great multitude, and "the land was filled with them."

The king feared that the Hebrews would become so strong that they would overthrow the Egyptians, and so escape from the land.

So the Egyptians appointed taskmasters, and made slaves of the children of Israel. And they were made to build great cities and monuments in the land.

"But the more they afflicted them, the more they multiplied and grew." The Egyptians did not know what to do with them.

Finally the king ordered that all the male children that were born should be put to death. But God cared for His people, and the order was not obeyed. And the number of the Israelites still increased.

Moses.

DURING these days of slavery a son was born to a family out of the tribe of Levi. His name was Moses. His mother loved him dearly. She determined that her baby should not be put to death as the king had commanded. So she hid him in her own house for three months.

But it was not safe to keep him at home any longer. So she made a little boat of rushes, and put him into it, and hid him in the flags by the river. His little sister Miriam was set to watch him.

One day the daughter of Pharaoh came with her servants to wash in the river. She found the little boat of bulrushes, and when it was opened she saw the babe.

Then Miriam came, and said, "Shall I go and call to thee a nurse of the Hebrew women?" "And Pharaoh's daughter said to her, Go." And she went and called the child's mother.

So the mother had the care of her son until he was old enough to go to the house of Pharaoh's daughter. And she adopted him as her son.

3

The Burning Bush.

*" And the angel of the Lord appeared unto him in a flame of fire out of the
midst of a bush."* Exodus 3 : 2.

ONE day, when Moses was forty years old, he went
out to see his brethren at their work. And he
saw an Egyptian beating one of his brethren. And
Moses slew the Egyptian.

When Pharaoh heard of it, he sought to slay
Moses. But Moses fled to the land of Midian. Here
he became a shepherd, and for forty years tended the
sheep of Jethro, priest of Midian.

One day while caring for the flocks, he saw a
strange sight. A bush was burning near him, but it
was not consumed. When he came near the bush, he
heard a voice, which said:—

"Put off thy shoes from off thy feet, for the place
whereon thou standest is holy ground."

It was the Lord speaking to him from the burning bush. And God told Moses that He had seen
the bondage of Israel in Egypt, and that the time had
now come for them to go free.

And the Lord told Moses to go to Egypt, and that
on the way he would meet his brother Aaron. They
were to go together to meet Pharaoh, and tell him that
God called upon him to let Israel go free.

Wonders in Egypt.

"And the Lord said unto Moses, When thou goest to return into Egypt, see that thou do all those wonders before Pharaoh." Exodus 4:21.

WHEN Moses and Aaron came before Pharaoh, they said, "Thus saith the Lord God of Israel, Let my people go."

"And Pharaoh said, Who is the Lord, that I should obey His voice to let Israel go? I know not the Lord, neither will I let Israel go."

Then the Lord sent wonders and plagues into Egypt, to subdue the stubborn heart of the king, and bring to the Egyptians the knowledge of the true God.

The first sign hurt no one. Aaron cast down his rod before Pharaoh, and it became a serpent. But the king hardened his heart, and refused to let Israel go. Then came ten terrible plagues upon the land.

You can read of them in Exodus, chapters six to eleven. They were so awful that almost everything was destroyed. But Pharaoh refused to let Israel go until the tenth plague.

In this last plague the oldest son in every house was slain. Then the king saw that he could not succeed in his rebellion against God, and he let Israel go.

At the Red Sea.

"And the Egyptians pursued, and went in after them. . . . And Moses stretched forth his hand over the sea. . . . And the waters returned, and covered the chariots; . . . there remained not so much as one of them." Exodus 14 : 23, 27, 28.

AFTER Israel had gone from Egypt, the king was sorry that he had let them go. They had been slaves, and he did not like to lose them.

So he took six hundred chariots and a great army, and started after the Israelites, to bring them back.

When Pharaoh and his army overtook them, they were completely hemmed in by mountains and the Red Sea. There seemed no way of escape.

But the Lord told Moses to stretch out his rod over the sea. And when he did so the waters parted, and became a wall on each side of them. And Israel passed over to the other side on dry ground.

Pharaoh and his army followed after Israel in the path the Lord had made through the sea. And the Lord hindered them by taking off their chariot wheels.

Then they became afraid, and tried to get back to land, but it was too late. The Lord told Moses to stretch forth his rod again. Then the waters returned, and drowned all the army of the Egyptians.

[36]

Bread from Heaven.

"Would to God we had died by the hand of the Lord in the land of Egypt, when we sat by the flesh pots, and when we did eat bread to the full; for ye have brought us forth into this wilderness, to kill this whole assembly with hunger." Exodus 16:3.

THE food which the people had brought with them from Egypt was almost gone. They did not see where they could get more.

So they complained to Moses, and said it would have been better if they had died by the plagues which God sent on Egypt, than to starve in the wilderness.

Then the Lord told Moses that He would send them bread from heaven. So each morning, when the dew was gone, the ground was covered with something white like frost. This was the bread which the Lord had promised them. And they called it manna.

Each morning they gathered just enough to last through the day, for it would not keep until the next morning.

But on the sixth day the Lord told them to gather enough for two days. The seventh day was the Sabbath, and no manna would fall on that day. By a miracle the Lord caused it to keep sweet and good through the Sabbath day.

So by two miracles each week God taught them about the Sabbath, and that He wanted them to keep it holy.

[37]

Quails.

"At even the quails came up, and covered the camp." Exodus 16:13.

WHEN God created man He gave him the food that was best for him. It was grains, vegetables, and the fruit of the trees. The Creator did not intend that man should kill animals, and use their flesh for food.

When Israel came out of Egypt the Lord gave them manna for food. It was a perfect, healthful food, especially when passing through the hot desert country.

But the Israelites had not traveled far until they began to long for the flesh pots of Egypt. So they complained to Moses, and the Lord sent them all the quails they could eat in a day.

About a year later they again complained bitterly. The Lord had given them the best food possible, but they despised it. "And the anger of the Lord was kindled greatly."

And He caused a strong wind to bring great numbers of quails. And the people stood up for two days and a night and gathered them. It is supposed they cured them in the hot sand so they would keep a long time.

And they ate quails for a whole month until they made them sick. And because of their rebellion the Lord sent a terrible plague among them.

[38]

Water from the Rock.

"And thou shalt smite the rock, and there shall come water out of it, that the people may drink." Exodus 17 : 6.

THE children of Israel had many difficulties and dangers to meet on the way from Egypt to Canaan.

The Lord had promised to help them on their journey, and He wanted them to learn to trust Him. But many times they complained when they came to any hard place.

When they pitched their camp at Rephidim there was no water, and they were very thirsty. And the people found fault with Moses for bringing them to such a place.

Then the Lord told Moses to go to a rock at Mount Horeb, and strike it with his rod. And when he did so there burst from it a stream of water, and the people had all they wanted.

This rock is an emblem of Christ. He is the Rock from which all spiritual blessings flow. This water is the "water of life." He will give it to all who thirst for it. Jesus has said, "Ho, every one that thirsteth, come ye to the waters." "If any man thirst, let him come unto Me, and drink." "And whosoever will, let him take the water of life freely."

Sinai.

"And the Lord came down upon Mount Sinai, . . . and the Lord called Moses up to the top of the mount." Exodus 19:20.

THE Israelites had been slaves to the heathen Egyptians for many years. During this time many of them had lost the knowledge of the true God. Hence on their journey the Lord gave them many lessons so that they might know and trust Him.

When they came to Sinai, the Lord called Moses to the top of the mountain. But the people were not to come near the mount, nor touch it, lest they die.

The mountain was a terrible sight to the people. It was covered with smoke, and there were thunders and lightnings, and an earthquake shook the mountain.

And the people were afraid, and fled from the mountain, and stood afar off. "And they said unto Moses, Speak thou with us, and we will hear: but let not God speak with us, lest we die."

Moses was forty days and forty nights with the Lord in the mount. While there the Lord told him how to build the tabernacle, and gave laws to govern the people.

And He gave Moses two tables of stone on which He had engraved the ten commandments, so that God's people should never again forget them.

"And thou shalt
teach them diligently unto
thy children, and shalt talk of them
when thou sittest in thine house, and when
thou walkest by the way, and when thou liest
down, and when thou risest up." Deut. 6:7.

THE LAW OF GOD

I

Thou shalt have no other gods before Me.

II

Thou shalt not make unto thee any graven image, or any likeness of any thing that is in heaven above, or that is in the earth beneath, or that is in the water under the earth: thou shalt not bow down thyself to them, nor serve them: for I the Lord thy God am a jealous God, visiting the iniquity of the fathers upon the children unto the third and fourth generation of them that hate Me; and shewing mercy unto thousands of them that love Me, and keep My commandments.

III

Thou shalt not take the name of the Lord thy God in vain; for the Lord will not hold him guiltless that taketh His name in vain.

IV

Remember the Sabbath day, to keep it holy. Six days shalt thou labour, and do all thy work: but the seventh day is the Sabbath of the Lord thy God: in it thou shalt not do any work, thou, nor thy son, nor thy daughter, thy manservant, nor thy maidservant, nor thy cattle, nor thy stranger that is within thy gates: for in six days the Lord made heaven and earth, the sea, and all that in them is, and rested the seventh day: wherefore the Lord blessed the Sabbath day, and hallowed it.

V

Honour thy father and thy mother: that thy days may be long upon the land which the Lord thy God giveth thee.

VI

Thou shalt not kill.

VII

Thou shalt not commit adultery.

VIII

Thou shalt not teal.

IX

Thou shalt not bear false witness against thy neighbour.

X

Thou shalt not covet thy neighbour's house, thou shalt not covet thy neighbour's wife, nor his manservant, nor his maidservant, nor his ox, nor his ass, nor any thing that is thy neighbour's.

"Think not that I am come to destroy the law, or the prophets: I am not come to destroy, but to fulfill. For verily I say unto you, Till heaven and earth pass, one jot or one tittle shall in no wise pass from the law, till all be fulfilled." Matthew 5:17, 18.

The Golden Calf.

"Up, make us gods, which shall go before us; for as for this Moses, . . . we wot not what is become of him." Exodus 32: 1.

AFTER Moses had been a long time in the mountain, the people became impatient. They did not want to wait so long for him.

So they came to Aaron, and told him to make them gods such as they had in Egypt. They thought if they had a god which they could see they could then go on to the promised land without Moses.

Aaron was afraid of the people, for they were a rebellious people. He was not firm like Moses. So he made them a golden calf. And they said, "These be thy gods, O Israel, which brought thee up out of the land of Egypt."

And the Lord told Moses what the people had done, and sent him down to them. And he met Joshua at the foot of the mount, and together they went to the camp.

When Moses saw them worshiping the calf he was very angry. And he threw down the tables of the law, and broke them. Then he took the calf, and burned it, and ground it to powder, and threw the powder into the water, and made the people drink of it.

Afterward the Lord again wrote the law on other tables of stone, and gave them to Moses.

The Tabernacle in the Wilderness.

"Let them make Me a Sanctuary; that I may dwell among them." Exodus 25: 8.

WHILE at Mount Sinai the children of Israel made the most wonderful building the world has ever seen. It was called the Tabernacle, and was to be used in the worship of God. The Lord told Moses just how to build it.

The Tabernacle was made like a tent. It was very beautiful. The pillars which held it up, and the boards for the sides, were covered with gold.

The inside of the roof was made of linen of different colors, the finest that could be made. Upon this covering pictures of cherubim were embroidered, worked with needle and thread.

Over this three other coverings were placed. One was made of goats' hair, another of rams' skins dyed red, and the last covering was of badgers' skins. These coverings were to keep out every particle of dust, and every drop of rain.

This Tabernacle is often called the Sanctuary. It had no windows, but was lighted by lamps, which burned day and night.

When the people moved on their journey, this Tabernacle was taken down and carried on the shoulders of men.

Outside the Tabernacle was an open court, around which was stretched a linen curtain. [43]

The Sanctuary.

" The vail shall divide unto you between the holy place and the most holy." Exodus 26 : 33.

THIS wonderful building was called the Tabernacle because it was made so that it could be taken down and moved from place to place.

It was also called the Sanctuary because it was the place where God came down and met with His people.

It was divided into two rooms by a curtain of fine linen. One room was the holy place, the other was the most holy.

Into the holy place came the priests every day to minister for the sins of the people. Into the most holy place the high priest alone could enter. He came once a year to atone before God for the sins of all Israel.

In the most holy place was the golden ark in which the tables of the law given on Mount Sinai were placed. In the holy place were the alter of incense, the golden candlestick, and the table of shewbread.

In the court, before the door of the Tabernacle, was placed the alter of burnt offering. On this altar was burned the animals slain to atone for the sins of the people.

As these offerings were made, the sinners were to remember that it was only through the death of Christ that they were to have full and final forgiveness and salvation.

[44]

The Twelve Spies.

" And the Lord spake unto Moses, saying, Send thou men, that they may search the land of Canaan." Numbers 13: 1, 2.

WHEN Israel came near to Canaan, the Lord told Moses to choose twelve men, one from each tribe, and send them to look over the land.

When they came back they said that the land was good. Among the fruit brought back was one cluster of grapes so large that two men carried it on a pole between them.

Then they spoiled all their good report by doubting the power of God to help them. They said that there were giants and strong nations in the land. "We be not able to go up against the people."

But two of the spies, Caleb and Joshua, were true, and said that with God's help they could go up and take the land. But the people believed the word of the unfaithful spies. And they complained to Moses and rebelled against God.

This rebellion showed that Israel was not then fit to go into the promised land. So the Lord sent them back into the wilderness, where they were to wander until all who came out of Egypt, except Caleb nd Joshua, should die. Forty years later their chil- en entered the land of Canaan.

Korah, Dathan, and Abiram.

"And the earth opened her mouth, and . . . they, and all that appertained to them, went
down alive into the pit, and the earth closed upon them." Numbers 16: 32, 33.

THE Lord had chosen Moses to be the leader of Israel.
He had chosen Aaron to be high priest. But Korah,
Dathan, and Abiram, and two hundred and fifty of the
princes of Israel, became jealous of them.

And they said, "Ye take too much upon you, seeing
all the congregation are holy."

This was a serious rebellion. If the congregation
should join in it, disaster would come to the whole camp.
So the Lord told Moses to separate the people from the
tents of the rebels. And the ground opened and swallowed
up the leaders, with their families, tents, and all they had.

And the Lord sent a fire among the two hundred
and fifty princes who had joined the rebellion, and
they were destroyed.

But rebellion was already in the camp. The next
day the people came to Moses and Aaron and said,
"Ye have killed the people of the Lord." Thus the
people charged Moses and Aaron with producing the
awful judgments which God had brought upon the rebels.

And the Lord sent a plague upon them which
destroyed fourteen thousand seven hundred people.

The Brazen Serpent.

"And the Lord sent fiery serpents among the people, and they bit the people; and much people of Israel died." Numbers 21:6.

THE children of Israel had many difficulties to meet on their journey from Egypt to the land of Canaan.

The Lord had promised to help them in all their troubles. But they did not trust Him, but complained and rebelled at every trial.

When they came to the land of Edom, which was near the promised land, they became discouraged because the way was not easy.

So they complained to Moses because there was not plenty of water. Of the manna sent from heaven they said, "Our soul loatheth this light bread."

This was a great sin. So the Lord let the fiery serpents of the wilderness come among them, and bite them. Very many died because of the serpents.

Then the people repented. Then the Lord told Moses to make a serpent of brass and put it upon a pole. And every one who was bitten was told to look at the serpent of brass, and all who looked were healed.

Jesus said, "As Moses lifted up the serpent in the wilderness, even so must the Son of man be lifted up." All who look to Jesus will be healed of their sins.

[47]

Joshua Made Leader of Israel.

"Take thee Joshua the son of Nun, a man in whom is the Spirit, and lay thine hand upon him." Numbers 27:18.

AFTER forty years of wandering in the wilderness, the Lord again undertook to bring the people into Canaan.

But as they came to Kadesh, very near the promised land, their supply of water ceased. And they complained again to Moses.

And the Lord told Moses to go to a rock that was near by, and speak to it, and water would come from it. Now Moses was a meek and patient man, but at this rebellion he became angry.

So, instead of speaking to the rock, as God had told him to do, he struck it twice with his rod, and said, "Hear now, ye rebels; must we fetch you water out of this rock?"

In this Moses took the glory to himself, and dishonored God. He thus set a wrong example before the people. And for this sin the Lord told him that he could not go with the people into the promised land.

So the Lord chose Joshua to lead Israel into the land of Canaan. Moses laid his hands upon him and ordained him for the great work before him.

The Death of Moses.

"So Moses the servant of the Lord died there in the land of Moab, according to the word of the Lord." Deuteronomy 34:5.

MOSES led the people till they came close to the borders of Canaan. Then the Lord said to him:—

"Get thee up into this mountain Abarim, unto Mount Nebo, which is in the land of Moab, that is over against Jericho; and behold the land of Canaan, which I give unto the children of Israel for a possession."

"Thou shalt see the land before thee; but thou shalt not go thither unto the land which I give the children of Israel."

And from the top of the mountain the Lord showed him the Land of Canaan which Israel was to have for their home. But because of his sin at Kadesh the Lord would not permit Moses to go with them.

"So Moses the servant of the Lord died there in the land of Moab, according to the word of the Lord.

"And He buried him in a valley in the land of Moab; . . . but no man knoweth of his sepulchre unto this day.

"And Moses was an hundred and twenty years old when he died; his eye was not dim, nor his natural force abated."

Crossing Over Jordan.

"And the priests that bear the ark of the covenant of the Lord stood firm on dry
ground in the midst of Jordan, and all the Israelites passed
over on dry ground." Joshua 3:17.

AFTER the death of Moses, Joshua led the people toward their new home in the land of Canaan. They were very glad to go into the promised land, for they had lived in the wilderness forty years.

When they came to the river Jordan they did not know how they could cross it. There was no bridge for them to cross, and there were no boats for so large a company.

But the Lord told Joshua what to do. So he had the people prepare to march, just as though there was no river in their way.

The priests went ahead with the ark of God, and the people followed after

And Joshua said to the priests, "When ye are come to the brink of the water of Jordan, ye shall stand still in Jordan."

And when the feet of the priests were dipped in the brink of the river, the water stopped flowing, and the bed of the river became dry. Then all the people crossed over on dry ground. And they camped "in the east border of Jericho."

Stones from the Jordan.

"Take you hence out of the midst of Jordan, . . . twelve stones, and ye shall carry them over with you." Joshua 4:3.

THE priests who carried the ark stopped in the middle of the Jordan, and waited there until all the hosts of Israel had crossed over.

Then twelve men, one from each tribe, picked up twelve stones from the bed of the river, and carried them over to the place where they were to camp that night. And they piled them up in a heap upon the bank of the river.

This pile of stones was to be a monument forever. And when the children should ask their parents what it meant, they should tell them the story of it.

"The waters of Jordan were cut off before the ark of the covenant of the Lord; when it passed over Jordan, . . . and these stones shall be for a memorial unto the children of Israel." Joshua 4:7.

How queer the river must have looked. On one side the waters were piled up in a heap extending back many miles. On the other side the bed of the river was dry farther than they could see.

As soon as the priests came out of the bed of the river the wall of water was broken, and the river ran on as before.

"And when the people shouted, the walls of Jericho
fell down flat."

The Fall of Jericho.

"So the people shouted when the priests blew with the trumpets; and . . . the wall fell down flat, so that the people went up into the city." Joshua 6:20.

THE land of Canaan was filled with wicked, heathen nations. So the Lord told Israel to destroy them, and take the country for their home.

The first city they came to was Jericho. It had strong, high walls all around it. The children of Israel could not take the city until these walls were thrown down.

God wanted to teach the nations of Canaan that He was fighting for His people. So He told Joshua just what to do.

Each day the people marched once around the city. The soldiers went first. Then came seven priests blowing trumpets of rams' horns. Next followed the ark, carried by priests. The people marched in silence after the ark.

On the seventh day they marched around the city seven times. Then the priests gave a long blast with their horns, and all the people shouted.

And when the people shouted, the walls of the city "fell down flat." Then the soldiers went into the city, and destroyed the wicked people as God had told them to do.

Gideon and His Army.

"By the three hundred men that lapped will I save you, and deliver the Midianites into thine hand." Judges 7:7.

AFTER the death of Joshua the people turned from the Lord and worshiped idols. Then the Lord permitted the heathen nations to afflict them and bring them into bondage.

Then Israel would cry to the Lord for help, and the Lord would choose them a judge who would deliver them, and teach them to serve the true God.

At one time the Lord chose Gideon to deliver His people from the Midianites. And he gathered an army of thirty-two thousand men.

And the Lord told Gideon that his army was too large. He told him to send home all who were afraid. And twenty-two thousand went home.

But the army was yet too large. God wanted all to know that He was working for His people. So He told Gideon to bring them to a brook to drink.

Every one who drank the water from his hand was to be taken, and those who bowed down and drank from the brook were to be sent home. Only three hundred drank from their hands. And these few Gideon led against their enemies.

[54]

Destruction of the Midianites.

"And they cried, The sword of the Lord, and of Gideon." Judges 7:20.

GIDEON armed his three hundred men in a very singular way. Each man carried in one hand a trumpet, and in the other a pitcher with a lamp in it. The pitchers would hide the lamps until they were ready to use them.

Then Gideon divided his little army into three companies of one hundred each. These little bands surrounded the entire camp of the Midianites.

When all was ready they broke their pitchers, blew their trumpets, and shouted, "The sword of the Lord and of Gideon."

The sound of the breaking pitchers, and the trumpets, and the shout of the men woke the camp of the Midianites. Then they saw in every direction the blaze of the lamps. It seemed to them that they were surrounded by a great army.

They became confused, and each man fought against his neighbor. And there was a very great slaughter.

When the tribes of Israel that were near heard of it they pursued the Midianites, and slew many more of them. One hundred and twenty thousand perished in this battle.

[55]

Samson and the Lion.

"And, behold, a young lion roared against him. And the Spirit of the Lord came mightily upon him, and he rent him as he would have rent a kid." Judges 14:5, 6.

MORE than a hundred years after the death of Gideon, the Philistines gained the victory over the Israelites, and oppressed them and afflicted them sore.

Then the Lord raised up Samson to deliver them. Now Samson was a very strong man, and did many wonderful things.

One day he was passing along on his way to a city of the Philistines, and a young lion came out to attack him. But the Lord helped him, and with his bare hands he slew the powerful beast.

At another time an army of the Philistines came against him. And he picked up a jaw bone of an ass, and with this queer weapon slew a thousand men.

At another time he went into Gaza, a city of the Philistines. This city had a strong wall around it, with very heavy gates through which the people went in and out.

And the people of Gaza shut the gates, so that Samson should not escape, for they wanted to kill him. But in the night Samson arose and pulled down one of the gates and carried it off on his back.

It was God who gave Samson this great strength.

The Death of Samson.

"The Philistines took him, and put out his eyes, and brought him down to Gaza, and bound him with fetters of brass; and he did grind in the prison house." Judges 16:21.

IN giving such great strength to Samson, the Lord commanded that the hair of his head should never be cut. If he disobeyed in this, his great strength would be taken from him.

So long as Samson obeyed God the Philistines could not take him. But he passed some of his time with wicked people. And one day when he was asleep a man came to him and cut off his hair, and his great strength left him.

Then the Philistines came in and bound him, and put out his eyes, and took him to Gaza, and made him grind in the mill of the prison.

While in the prison his hair grew again, and his strength came back to him.

One day the Philistines had a great feast in the temple of their god Dagon. And they brought in Samson so that they might rejoice over him. But they did not know that his strength had returned to him.

And Samson took hold of the two great pillars which held up the building, and tore them down. Thousands of the Philistines were killed in the fall of the building, and Samson died with them.

Eli and Samuel.

"And the Lord came, and stood, and called as at other times, Samuel, Samuel. Then Samuel answered, Speak; for Thy servant heareth." 1 Samuel 3:10.

ELI was a priest of the Lord and Judge of Israel. He was an old man, and his sons were very wicked. And there was a little boy who lived with Eli. His name was Samuel, and he helped in the work of the sanctuary.

One night when Samuel had lain down to sleep he heard some one call him. He thought Eli had called him, so he ran to him, and said, "Here am I."

But Eli answered, "I called not; lie down again." So Samuel went back to his bed.

Again the Lord called, "Samuel," and again he ran to Eli, and said, "Here am I; for thou didst call me."

Then Eli knew that the Lord had called Samuel. So he said, "Go, lie down: and it shall be, if He call thee, that thou shalt say, Speak, Lord; for thy servant heareth."

And the Lord called the third time, and Samuel answered as Eli had told him. Then the Lord told Samuel that the family of Eli should not remain as priests of the Lord, because the sons of Eli were wicked men, and Eli had not restrained them.

Saul Made King of Israel.

"Now make us a king to judge us like all the nations." 1 Samuel 8:5.

AT the death of Eli Samuel became judge of Israel. He was also a priest and prophet of the Lord.

When he became an old man the elders of Israel came to him and said, "Make us a king to judge us like all the nations."

Before this they were different from the other nations. The Lord Himself had taken care of them. And He had given them judges and prophets to rule them, and tell them what the Lord wanted them to do.

But they were not pleased with the Lord's plan. They wanted to have a king, and be like the nations around them.

But the thing displeased Samuel. He knew it was not best for them. But the Lord told him to listen to the people, and do as they had asked, and make them a king.

And the Lord chose Saul to be their first king. So Samuel took a vial of oil and poured it upon his head, and anointed him, and told him that he was to be king of Israel.

But after Saul was made king he became proud and disobeyed the Lord, and did many wicked things.

David and Goliath.

" And David said to Saul, . . . Thy servant will go and fight with this Philistine." 1 Samuel 17: 32.

NOW the Philistines came up to fight with Saul. And Jesse, who lived at Bethlehem, had two sons in Saul's army. So he sent his youngest son, David, to see if they were well.

While David was in the camp with his brothers, the giant Goliath came from the camp of the Philistines, and cried out to the men of Saul's army. He called on them to send a man to fight with him. But they were afraid, and no one dared to go.

And David said, "Who is this . . . Philistine, that he should defy the armies of the living God?"

And they took him to Saul. And David said, "I will go and fight with this Philistine."

And David went to a brook, and picked out five small stones, and he ran to meet Goliath. When he came near he put one of the stones in his sling, and threw it at the giant. And the stone hit him in the forehead and killed him.

Then the army of the Philistines fled. And Saul's army pursued them, and gained a great victory.

David Plays Before Saul.

" And David came to Saul, and . . . took an harp, and played with his hand : so Saul was refreshed." 1 Samuel 16:21, 23.

AFTER the death of Goliath David became a general in the army of Saul. And the Lord prospered whatever he did. But Saul was filled with pride, and did not obey the Lord. So the Spirit of the Lord left him.

Saul knew that he was not right with God, but he was stubborn and determined to have his own way. His thoughts troubled him, and he became cross and sullen.

Now David could play beautifully on the harp. So when Saul was feeling bad they would call David to play before the king, and he would feel better.

But Saul was very jealous. So when the people praised David, Saul became very angry, and tried to kill him.

So David fled from Saul, and lived in the wilderness, and in the dens and caves of the mountains. And many men came to him, and he soon had an army of six hundred men.

Whenever Saul could learn where David was, he would come with an army to take him. But the Lord cared for David, and always warned him so that he could escape.

The Death of Saul.

"So Saul died, and his three sons, and his armorbearer, and all his men, that same day together." 1 Samuel 31:6.

SAUL had spent much of his time hunting for David. In doing this he had neglected the care of his own kingdom.

The Philistines knew this, and came against Israel with a great army. Before Saul could meet and stop them, they had come into the very heart of the kingdom of Israel.

Saul's army was small, and the army of the Philistines was very large. If Saul and his people had been right with God the matter of numbers would have made no difference.

But Saul had sinned, and had led Israel into sin. So when they asked the Lord to tell them what to do, as they had in the past, He would not answer them. So they knew that the Lord would not help them.

A bloody battle was soon fought, and the army of Saul was defeated. Three of the Sons of Saul were killed. Saul himself was wounded, so that he could neither fight nor escape.

He did not want to fall into the hands of the wicked Philistines, so he asked his armorbearer to kill him, but he would not. So he fell on his own sword, and died.

David Made King.

WHEN the Lord rejected Saul, He chose David to be the next king. But David was a very young man when the Lord chose him. It was years before Saul died and David began his reign.

After the death of Saul, David went up to Hebron, and was crowned king over the tribe of Judah. But the rest of the tribes of Israel took Ish-bosheth, the son of Saul, and made him their king.

Ish-bosheth reigned two years, and then was killed. Then all the tribes of Israel came to David and joined in making him king of all Israel. Thus God's plan in making David king was carried out.

At this time the kingdom of Israel was not strong. The nations around were continually making war upon Israel, and the people were in trouble and distress.

But David did what was right, and the Lord blessed him in all that he did. He soon conquered the nations around him, and the land had rest from all their enemies.

David was thirty years old when he began to reign, and he reigned forty years.

Solomon Builds the Temple.

"I have surely built Thee an house to dwell in." 1 Kings 8:13.

AT the death of David his son Solomon was made king. And Solomon asked the Lord to give him wisdom, and the request pleased the Lord. And He gave him wisdom, and riches, and peace from his enemies.

But the worship of God was still carried on in a tent. So Solomon built a splended temple to take the place of the tent. When completed it was one of the finest buildings in the world.

The Sanctuary where the priests' services were carried on, was a most beautiful place. It was divided into two rooms, called the holy and the most holy place.

The walls of these rooms were of cedar, beautifully carved, and overlaid with pure gold. Even the floors were overlad with gold. These rooms had no windows, but were lighted by a golden lamp which had branches. These lights were kept burning day and night. The effect of this light on the walls of gold was very beautiful.

When the temple was finished there was a great gathering of the people and a solemn dedication. Read Solomon's prayer in 1 Kings 8.

[64]

Solomon and the Queen of Sheba.

"When the queen of Sheba heard of the fame of Solomon concerning the name of the Lord, she came to prove him with hard questions." 1 Kings 10: 1.

AFTER Solomon had been made king, the Lord appeared to him at Gibeon in a dream, and said to him, "Ask what I shall give thee."

And Solomon answered, "Give therefore Thy servant an understanding heart to judge Thy people, that I may discern between good and bad."

This answer pleased the Lord. And He said to Solomon that He would give him wisdom as he had asked, and also riches and honor among the nations.

The fame of Solomon went everywhere. And the queen of Sheba heard of him. So she came to the court of Solomon, and asked him hard questions. And he answered them every one.

She saw also his riches, and the greatness of his kingdom. Then she said to him that she had heard wonderful things about him, but "the half was not told me."

But when Solomon was old he turned from the Lord and worshiped idols. For this sin the Lord told him that when he died his kingdom would be divided, and the only part left to his house would be the tribe of Judah.

5

Elijah and King Ahab.

"And Elijah . . . said unto Ahab, As the Lord God of Israel liveth, . . . there shall not be dew nor rain these years, but according to my word." 1 Kings 17:1.

AHAB was the wickedest king that ever reigned in Israel. He worshiped idols, and led Israel into sin.

Elijah was a prophet of God, and was grieved at the wicked ways of Ahab, and for the sins of the people.

Finally the Lord sent him to tell the king that because of the sins of Israel no more rain would fall upon the land until Elijah should pray the Lord to send it.

Then the Lord sent Elijah to another country, where Ahab could not find him. And he dwelt beside the brook Chereth. And the Lord commanded the ravens, and they brought him food twice every day.

But by-and-by the waters of the brook became dry. Then the Lord sent Elijah to Zarepath, where He provided him food in the house of a widow.

After three years and a half of famine, the Lord sent Elijah to meet Ahab. And he told the king to prepare for rain. Then the prophet went to the top of mount Carmel and prayed seven times. In answer to his prayer it rained so hard that Ahab could hardly get to his home.

[66]

Elijah and the Chariot of Fire.

"There appeared a chariot of fire, and horses of fire, and parted them both asunder; and Elijah went up by a whirlwind into heaven." 2 Kings 2:11.

ELIJAH served the Lord faithfully, and the Lord would take him to heaven without dying.

And the Lord chose Elisha to be prophet when Elijah should be taken away. So he forsook his work and his home and followed Elijah.

And they traveled together until they came to the River Jordan. And Elijah folded up his mantel and smote the waters. And the waters parted, and they went over on dry ground.

And Elijah said to Elisha, "Ask what I shall do for thee." And Elisha answered, "Let a double portion of thy spirit be upon me."

Then said Elijah, "Thou hast asked a hard thing: nevertheless, if thou see me when I am taken from thee, it shall be so unto thee."

As they talked, there appeared a chariot of fire, and Elijah was taken up in a whirlwind.

"And Elisha saw it, and he cried, My father, my father, the chariot of Israel, and the horsemen thereof." And he found the mantel of Elijah which had fallen from him. And the Spirit of the Lord came upon him, and he became one of the greatest prophets of Israel.

Elisha and the Widow's Oil.

"Go, sell the oil, and pay thy debt." 2 Kings 4:7.

THERE are many wonderful things in the life of Elisha. He was a true servant of God, and He blessed him in whatever he did.

At one time Naaman the Syrian came to be healed of the leprosy. And Elisha told him to dip seven times in the Jordan. And when he did so he was healed.

In Shunem there was a house where Elisha would often stop as he passed by. And they built him a room, and cared for him whenever he came. And it came to pass that the son of the Shunammite died, and Elisha came and prayed to God for him, and he was raised to life.

At another time a widow was in great trouble. She was in debt to a hard man, and he was coming to take her two boys and sell them as slaves. And she cried to Elisha, and he told her to go to her neighbors and borrow all the dishes she could.

All she had in the house was a pot of oil. And Elisha told her to pour it into the dishes she had borrowed. And she filled one dish, and then another until all the dishes were full. And she sold the oil and paid her debt, and her sons were not taken from her.

Israel Taken to Babylon.

"And this whole land shall be a desolation, and an astonishment; and these nations shall serve the king of Babylon seventy years.' Jeremiah 25: 11.

THE Lord gave to the children of Israel beautiful homes in the land of Canaan. So long as they lived right and obeyed Him, He took care of them and protected them from their enemies.

But when Israel sinned and worshipped idols instead of the Lord, He could not protect them. Then their enemies would come against them and afflict them.

When the Jews were in trouble they would return to the Lord and pray to Him for help. Then He would drive away their enemies and again give them peace in all their land.

But in the days of Isaiah and Jeremiah the people became very wicked and would not return to the Lord. The Lord sent prophets to warn them but they would not listen to them, and tried to kill them.

It was then that Nebuchadnezzar, king of Babylon, sent a great army to fight against the people of Israel.

When the armies of Babylon came to Jerusalem, they had a long, hard battle, but finally broke down the wall and took the city. Then they made captives of the people and carried them to Babylon.

A Temperance Lesson.

"But Daniel purposed in his heart that he would not defile himself with the portion of the king's meat, nor with the wine which he drank." Daniel 1:8.

KING Nebuchadnezzar chose some of the best of the young men from among the captives of Israel. He gave them the same food which he ate, and educated them in his court. He wanted them to be fitted to help in the government of his kingdom.

Among them were Daniel, Hananiah, Mishael, and Azariah. They were from the king's family in Judah. But they found that wine and many things which God had forbidden them to eat, were in the food provided by the king.

These young men determined that they would not disobey God by eating and drinking these things. So Daniel said, "Let them give us pulse to eat, and water to drink."

After a trial of ten days they looked so well that their keeper consented to let them have the food they desired. And God blessed them because of their obedience, and "gave them knowledge and skill in all learning and wisdom."

At the end of three years the king examined all the young men. "And among them all was found none like Daniel, Hananiah, Mishael, and Azariah: therefore stood they before the king."

Nebuchadnezzar's Dream.

"Thou, O king, sawest, and behold a great image." Daniel 2:31.

ONE night king Nebuchadnezzar dreamed a wonderful dream. But when he awoke he could not remember it.

There were men in Babylon who claimed that they could tell secrets, and he called them in. But they could not tell the king his dream.

Then the king was very angry, and commanded that all the wise men of Babylon should be put to death. But Daniel asked them to wait and he would tell the king his dream.

Then Daniel and his three friends prayed earnestly, and the Lord told Daniel all about it. And he came to the king, and said:—

"Thou, O king, sawest, and behold a great image." Its head was of gold, its breast and arms were of silver, its sides of brass, and its legs of iron.

He told the king that this represented four great kingdoms that would rule the whole world. He told the king that his kingdom was the head of gold.

Three others were to follow, and then the God of heaven would set up a kingdom that would last forever.

Pages 95 and 96 of this book tell about this kingdom.

The Fiery Furnace.

"Then these men were bound, . . . and were cast into the midst of the burning fiery furnace." Daniel 3:21.

NEBUCHADNEZZAR was a heathen king. So he made a great image of gold. It was to represent the god which he worshiped. It was ninety feet tall, and nine feet wide across the shoulders.

Then the king gathered together the great men of his kingdom to worship this image. Among them were Hananiah, Mishael, and Azariah. But the king had given them new names. Hananiah he called Shadrach, Mishael he called Meshach, and Azariah he called Abed-nego.

Nebuchadnezzar commanded that when the music should play every one should fall down and worship the image. But the three Israelites would not worship the idol.

Then the king was very furious, and had them cast into an awful furnace of fire. But the Lord took care of them, and they walked in the fire as if they were in the open air. Then the king had them taken out, and there was not even the smell of fire on them.

By this wonderful miracle the Lord was teaching these heathen that the God of heaven was the only true God, and He could care for His servants.

The Handwriting on the Wall.

" In the same hour came forth fingers of a man's hand, and wrote . . . upon the plaster of the wall of the king's palace." Daniel 5:5.

NOW Nebuchadnezzar was dead, and Belshazzar, his grandson, was king in Babylon. And Belshazzar made a feast to a thousand of his lords. And he had brought in the golden vessels taken by Nebuchadnezzar from the temple of the Lord at Jerusalem.

This was done to insult and defy the God of Israel. "They drank wine, and praised the gods of gold, and of silver, of brass, of iron, of wood, and of stone."

But the Lord took notice of it, and in the same hour there came the fingers of a man's hand, writing on the wall. Then the whole company was frightened, and their knees smote together.

Then the king called in his wise men, but they could not tell the meaning of the words on the wall. At last Daniel came in. He told them of the true God, and how they had insulted Him. And he told them what the handwriting meant.

"MENE; God hath numbered thy kingdom and finished it. TEKEL; Thou art weighed in the balances, and art found wanting. PEREZ; Thy kingdom is divided and given to the Medes and Persians."

That night the city was taken by the army of the Medes and Persians as the writing had said.

IN THE DEN OF LIONS.

Daniel Prays to God.

"Then the king commanded, and they brought Daniel, and cast him into the den of lions." Daniel 6:16.

BABYLON had now become a Medo-Persian kingdom. Daniel had been made the highest officer in the kingdom. The other officers did not like to have an Israelite over them. So they laid a trap to destroy him because of his worship of the true God.

So one day they asked king Darius to make a decree that for thirty days no one should pray to any god, or ask anything of any man but of the king. If any one disobeyed this decree, he was to be cast into the den of lions.

The king made the decree. But Daniel prayed three times a day as usual. And he did not even shut his windows.

The men were watching, and told the king. The king could not change his decree, and so Daniel was cast into the den of lions. But the Lord cared for Daniel, and shut the mouths of the lions so they could not hurt him.

The next morning Daniel was taken out of the den, and the wicked officers were cast in, and were destroyed at once.

Cradled in a Manger.

"And she . . . wrapped Him in swaddling clothes, and laid Him in a manger."
Luke 2:7.

THE Roman emperor had commanded that all the world should be taxed. So Joseph and Mary came to Bethlehem, the city of David, to have their names enrolled.

It was a long, weary journey from their home in Nazareth to Bethlehem. How glad they must have been when they came in sight of the place. Here they expected to find rest in the inn.

But every room was taken by others. The only place where they could rest was in a stable. And here Jesus our Lord was born, with a manger for His cradle. Yet He was the Son of God, the creator of the world.

Of His birth the prophet Isaiah wrote, "Unto us a child is born, unto us a son is given: and the government shall be upon His shoulder: and His name shall be called Wonderful, Counsellor, The mighty God, The everlasting Father, The Prince of Peace." Isaiah 9:6.

If the people of Bethlehem had only known who this babe was which was so humbly born, how they would have opened their doors and welcomed Him!

What the Shepherds Saw.

"For unto you is born this day in the city of David a Saviour, which is Christ
the Lord." Luke 2:11.

AND there were in the same country shepherds abiding in the field, keeping watch over their flock by night.

"And, lo, the angel of the Lord came upon them, and the glory of the Lord shone round about them: and they were sore afraid.

"And the angel said unto them, Fear not: for, behold, I bring you good tidings of great joy, which shall be to all people.

"For unto you is born this day in the city of David a Saviour, which is Christ the Lord.

"And this shall be a sign unto you; Ye shall find the babe wrapped in swaddling clothes, lying in a manger.

"And suddenly there was with the angel a multitude of the heavenly host praising God, and saying,

"Glory to God in the highest, and on earth peace, good will toward men."

"And they came with haste, and found Mary and Joseph, and the babe lying in a manger."

"And the shepherds returned, glorifying and praising God for all the things that they had heard and seen." Luke 2:8–20.

A New Star.

"We have seen His star in the East and are come to worship Him." Matthew 2: 2.

IN the East, far away from Jerusalem, lived some men who were very wise. These men had learned that Jesus was soon coming to earth.

The Spirit of the Lord had told them that when Jesus came they would see a bright, new star. If they would follow this star it would take them to Him.

One night, as they were studying the heavens, they saw this new star. They started toward it, and it led them to Jerusalem.

There they came to King Herod and asked, "Where is He that is born king of the Jews?"

Herod called together the wise men of Israel, and asked where Christ should be born. And they answered, "In Bethlehem."

Then Herod sent the wise men to Bethlehem. He told them to come back and tell him when they found Jesus, so that he could go and worship Him also. But he wanted to know where He was so he could kill Him.

When the wise men started, the star again appeared, and led them to the stable where the Saviour lay. And they worshiped Him, and gave Him many costly presents.

[78]

Going Down to Egypt.

"Arise, and take the young child and His mother, and flee into Egypt." Matthew 2: 13.

THE Lord came to the wise men in a dream and told them not to go back to Herod at Jerusalem. So they went home another way.

"And when they were departed, behold, the angel of the Lord appeared to Joseph in a dream, saying, Arise, and take the young child and His mother, and flee into Egypt, and be thou there until I bring thee word: For Herod will seek the young child to destroy Him."

And Joseph did as the Lord told him. Now Joseph was a poor man. But the splendid gifts made by the wise men, of gold and costly spices, paid the expense of the journey, and the cost of living while they were in Egypt.

When the wise men did not return to Herod, he was very angry. And he sent and killed all the childr n cf Bethlehem who were not more than two years old.

By doing this Herod was sure that Jesus would be killed with the other children. But His heavenly Father cared for Him. At the death of Herod they all returned to Nazareth.

[79]

Going Up to Jerusalem.

"And when He was twelve years old, they went up to Jerusalem after the custom of the feast." Luke 2:42.

ONCE each year all the people went up to Jerusalem to the feast of the passover.

When Jesus was twelve years old, Joseph and Mary took Him with them when they went up to this feast. It came in the spring, and many families traveled together. This made it a pleasant journey from Nazareth to Jerusalem.

When the feast was over, Joseph and Mary started for their home. They joined the company of others who were going the same road. But Jesus did not go with them.

Although they did not see Jesus as they left Jerusalem, they supposed He was somewhere in the company. But when night came and they could not find Him, they were much troubled.

The next morning they started back, hoping to find Him on the way, but could see no trace of Him. They thought of how careless they had been, and feared that some harm had come to Him.

After three days they found Him in the temple among the great teachers of Israel.

Among the Doctors in the Temple.

"They found Him in the temple, sitting in the midst of the doctors, both hearing them, and asking them questions." Luke 2:46.

JESUS had never before seen the temple. In going from place to place, and watching the services of the priests, He became separated from His parents.

He finally came to a room where the rabbis were teaching the Bible to the youth. Here He sat and listened to the teaching, and asked them questions. They soon saw that He understood the Bible better than they did.

When His parents found Him, Mary said to Him, "Son, why hast Thou thus dealt with us? behold, Thy father and I have sought Thee sorrowing.

"And He said unto them, How is it that ye sought Me? wist ye not that I must be about My father's business?"

6

"And He went down with them, and came to Nazareth, and was subject unto them. . . . And Jesus increased in wisdom and stature, and in favor with God and man." Luke 2 : 51, 52.

The Baptism of Jesus.

"Then cometh Jesus from Galilee to Jordan unto John, to be baptized of him." Matthew 3:13.

JOHN the Baptist was sent by the Lord to prepare the way for the Saviour. His home was in the wilderness, near the River Jordan. The people came long distances to hear him preach.

He preached that "the kingdom of God is at hand." He called upon the people to repent and be baptized.

When Jesus was about thirty years of age He came to the Jordan to be baptized by John. He was not baptized because He was a sinner, but to set an example for us to follow.

John did not feel worthy to baptize Jesus, and said, "I have need to be baptized of Thee, and cometh Thou to me?"

Jesus answered, "Suffer it to be so now: for thus it becometh us to fulfil all righteousness." And he baptized Him.

When they came up out of the water, the heavens were opened, and the Spirit of God, in the form of a dove, came down and rested upon Jesus.

And they heard a voice from heaven, saying, "This is My beloved Son, in whom I am well pleased."

Turning Water Into Wine.

"Jesus saith unto them, Fill the waterpots with water." John 2:7.

SOON after His baptism Jesus returned to Galilee. Here He and His mother were invited to the marriage of one of their friends, at the little village of Cana.

At this wedding they had a feast at which they used wine. But they had not provided enough, and the mother of Jesus said to Him, "They have no wine."

Then she turned to the servants and said, "Whatsoever He saith unto you, do it."

Near-by there were six waterpots of stone. They would each hold about five or six pailfuls.

Then Jesus said to the servants, "Fill the waterpots with water."

When they were full He said to them, "Draw out now, and bear unto the governor of the feast."

The governor did not know that the wine was made by Jesus, but as soon as he tasted it he found that it was better than any wine that they had been drinking.

The wine that Jesus made was the pure, sweet juice of the grape, and could not make any one drunk. Isaiah calls this "the new wine . . . in the cluster."

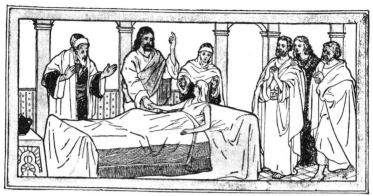

Healing the Sick.

"And He took the damsel by the hand, and said unto her, Talitha cuma; which is, being interpreted, Damsel, I say unto thee, arise." Mark 5:41.

WHEREVER Jesus went the sick, the blind, the deaf, and the lame were brought to Him, and He healed them all.

One day Jairus, a ruler of the synagogue, came to Him and said, "My little daughter lieth at the point of death: I pray Thee, come and lay Thy hands on her, that she may be healed; and she shall live."

It was a long way to the ruler's house, and before they came to it they met some people from the bedside of the young girl, who said to the ruler, "Thy daughter is dead."

Jesus heard these words, and said to the ruler, "Be not afraid, only believe."

And Jesus took Peter, James, and John, and went with the ruler into his house. There He found women weeping and wailing according to the custom of that country. And He put them out of the room where the child lay.

Then Jesus took the maid by the hand, and told her to arise. "And straightway the damsel arose, and walked; for she was of the age of twelve years. And they were astonished with a great astonishment."

Jesus Feeds the Five Thousand.

"He said unto them, Give ye them to eat." Luke 9:13.

JESUS had been teaching the people in a desert place near Bethsaida. They had had no food all day, and the disciples asked Him to send them away that they might go into the villages around and buy food and find a place to stay through the night.

Jesus knew that many would suffer if He sent them away hungry. So He said to the disciples, "Give ye them to eat."

But there were five thousand to be fed, and they had only five loaves and two small fishes. But Jesus knew what He would do.

He told the disciples to make the people sit down on the grass in companies of fifty. Then He took the bread and fishes, and looking up to heaven blessed them. Then He brake them, and gave to the disciples, and they carried the food to the people sitting in companies.

And they all ate as much as they wanted. And when they were through, Jesus said, "Gather up the fragments that remain, that nothing be lost."

And when they had gathered the fragments, they had twelve baskets full.

[86]

A Sabbath Lesson.

"The Sabbath was made for man." Mark 2:27.

WHEN Jesus was upon earth there were but few who had the love of God in their hearts. Many of the Jews were proud and cruel. They were unkind to the poor, and had little sympathy for the suffering.

But they professed to be very pious, and had many outward forms, which led others to think they were very holy. Especially were they very strict about keeping the Sabbath.

Sometimes Jesus would heal the sick on the Sabbath. Then the proud Pharisees would be angry, and accuse Him of breaking the Sabbath.

One Sabbath Jesus and His disciples were passing through a field of grain. The disciples had been without food for a long time, and were hungry. So they plucked and ate some of the ears of grain.

This made the Pharisees angry, and they said, "Behold, Thy disciples do that which is not lawful to do upon the Sabbath day."

Then Jesus told them that "the Sabbath was made for man." It was made to be a blessing and not a burden. At another time He told them that it was lawful to do good on the Sabbath.

Jesus and the Children.

"Suffer the little children to come unto Me, and forbid them not: for of such is the kingdom of God." Mark 10:14.

JESUS loved the children. Their innocence and purity were dear to His heart. He was glad to have the mothers bring them for Him to heal and bless.

One day, after Jesus had been teaching for a long time, some fond mothers brought their children to Jesus. How happy they would be if He would heal and bless them.

The disciples knew that Jesus was very weary, so they told the mothers that they should not trouble the Master at such a time.

"But when Jesus saw it, He was much displeased, and said unto them, Suffer the little children to come unto Me, and forbid them not: for of such is the kingdom of God."

At another time He said, "Except ye be converted, and become as little children, ye shall not enter into the kingdom of heaven."

[88]

Riding into Jerusalem.

"A very great multitude spread their garments in the way; others cut down branches from the trees, and strewed them in the way." Matthew 21 : 8.

JESUS was coming up to Jerusalem to eat His last Passover supper. His work on earth was nearly done. He knew that before the feast was ended He would be crucified.

But the people thought He was coming to Jerusalem to be made king of Israel. So they spread their garments in the way, and laid before Him branches of the olive- and palm-trees, and shouted:—

"Hosanna to the Son of David! Blessed is He that cometh in the name of the Lord! Hosanna in the highest!"

Never before had Jesus permitted His followers to treat Him as a king. He said, "My kingdom is not of this world." But now, as His work was closing, He desired that as many as possible should know of Him and His mission to earth.

The Betrayal.

"Jesus said unto him, Judas, betrayest thou the Son of man with a kiss?"
Luke 22:48.

AFTER eating the Passover supper, Jesus and the disciples went to the Mount of Olives. Here He prayed earnestly to His Father. He knew the terrible death He must die, and wanted help.

While He was praying the disciples slept, for they were weary. After His prayer, Jesus said to them, "Rise, let us be going: behold, he is at hand that doth betray Me.

"And while He yet spake, lo, Judas, one of the twelve, came, and with him a great multitude with swords and staves, from the chief priests and elders of the people."

Many of the mob did not know Jesus. So Judas had said to them, "Whomsoever I shall kiss, that same is He: hold Him fast.

"And forthwith he came to Jesus, and said, Hail Master; and kissed Him."

"Jesus said unto him, Judas, betrayest thou the Son of man with a kiss?"

And "all the disciples forsook Him, and fled." Then they took Jesus and brought Him to the chief priests and rulers.

The Crucifixion.

"And they crucified Him, and parted His garments, casting lots." Matthew 27 : 35.

THE Jews wanted to kill Jesus, but the Romans would not permit them to put any man to death. So they took Him to Pilate, the Roman governor.

Here they accused Him of many things, but could prove none of them. Some of His accusers shouted one thing and some another, but all united in crying that Jesus should be put to death.

A great mob was gathered, and they all cried, "Crucify Him, crucify Him." They hated Him because He reproved them for their sins.

Pilate did not believe that Jesus had done any wrong, but he was a coward. So he did what the Jews asked him to do. He sentenced Jesus to be crucified.

So they took Him to a mountain outside of Jerusalem, called Calvary, and crucified Him between two thieves. It was an awful death to die.

We are all sinners, and Paul says, "The wages of sin is death." But Jesus came to save all who would come to Him. All who believe in Jesus will be saved in His kingdom when He comes to earth again.

The Resurrection.

"He is not here: for He is risen, as He said. Come, see the place where the Lord lay." Matthew 28:6.

AFTER Jesus died, Joseph, a Jewish ruler who believed on Jesus, took His body and laid it in a new tomb. A stone was then rolled before the door. Roman soldiers were sent to watch and see that no one should take His body away.

But early on the first day of the week a bright angel came to the tomb. He rolled away the stone from the tomb, and cried:—

"Jesus, Thou Son of God, Thy Father calls Thee."

As the Roman guard saw the brightness of the angel, they fell as dead men to the ground, and there was a great earthquake. Then Jesus came forth from the tomb, never to die again.

As Jesus was raised from the dead, so will all who believe in Him be raised when He comes again. See 1 Corinthians 15:12–18.

The good who are thus raised from the dead, will never die again. They will live forever in a beautiful home which God will give them. In that home there will be no sin, sickness, pain, nor sorrow. All will be happy forever.

Jesus Meets His Disciples.

"They saw a fire of coals there, and fish laid thereon, and bread. . . . Jesus saith
unto them, Come and dine." John 21 : 9, 12.

AFTER the resurrection Jesus was seen first by Mary Magdalene at the sepulchre. Next He appeared to the two disciples who were on their way to Emmaus.

That same night the disciples were in a room, and the door was locked. All at once they saw Jesus in their midst, and were afraid. But He said, "Peace be unto you." After eight days He again met them.

After this the disciples went back to their homes in Galilee. Some of them were fishermen.

So one evening Peter said, "I go a fishing."

The others said, "We also go with thee."

They fished all night, but caught nothing, so they started for the shore. As they came near they saw Jesus waiting for them, but did not know Him.

Then He called to them, and said, "Cast the net on the right side of the ship, and ye shall find."

They did so, and caught a hundred and fifty-three nice large fishes. Then they knew it was Jesus.

And when they came to the shore there was a fire, and nicely roasted fish, and bread. And Jesus said, "Come and dine."

Jesus Goes Back to Heaven.

"And . . . while they beheld, He was taken up; and a cloud received Him out of their sight." Acts 1 : 9.

WHEN the work of Jesus upon earth was finished, He walked with His disciples to the Mount of Olives. Here He talked with them for the last time, and told them what they should do. He was about to leave them, but they did not know it.

As He ceased talking, He reached out His hands and blessed them, and began to rise from them into the air. Higher and higher He went from them, until He entered a cloud and they saw Him no more. This was a cloud of angels who had come to go with Him on His way back to His Father in heaven.

The disciples stood in wonder and sorrow, for their Lord had left them. As they still gazed into the sky where Jesus had disappeared, they heard a voice by their side, and they looked and saw two angels standing by them, who said:—

"Ye men of Galilee, why stand ye gazing up into heaven? this same Jesus, which is taken up from you into heaven, shall so come in like manner as ye have seen Him go into heaven." Acts 1 : 11.

And they returned to Jerusalem comforted.

[94]

I Will Come Again.

"I will come again, and receive you unto Myself; that where I am, there ye may be also." John 14:3.

THE second coming of Christ to earth is the hope of every Christian. Paul said, "And unto them that look for Him shall He appear the second time." Hebrews 9:28.

The angels told the disciples that "this same Jesus" shall come again.

How will He come to earth again? "In like manner as ye have seen Him go into heaven," said the angels.

They saw Him as He ascended. John says that when He comes back "every eye shall see Him." Revelation 1:7.

"A cloud received Him out of their sight," when He went away. He will come back the same way, for we read, "Behold, He cometh with clouds." All the angels of heaven will come with Him. See Matthew 25:31.

Jesus is not to come in a silent, or secret manner. He says, "For as the lightning cometh out of the east, and shineth even unto the west; so shall also the coming of the Son of man be." Matthew 24:27.

When Jesus comes He will reward all who have been good and true, for He says, "Behold, I come quickly; and My reward is with Me, to give every man according as his work shall be." Revelation 22:12.

The Earth Made New.

"Behold, I create new heavens and a new earth." Isaiah 65:17.

THIS earth is not as it was when God first made it. Then it was beautiful and perfect, for God Himself said "it was very good." Genesis 1:31.

But the earth now has barren, rocky waste places, and great oceans covering more than half of it. There is now much sin and sorrow and pain in the earth.

The apostle Peter says there will be "a new earth' by and by. 2 Peter 3:13. It will be just as beautiful as it was when it was first made.

There will be no sin nor sorrow there, for John says, "And God shall wipe away all tears from their eyes; and there shall be no more death, neither sorrow, nor crying, neither shall there be any more pain." Revelation 21:4.

The animals will not be savage and ugly in our new earth home, for "The wolf also shall dwell with the lamb, and the leopard shall lie down with the kid; and the calf and the young lion and the fatling together; and a little child shall lead them." Isaiah 11:6.